Contents

KU-147-637

Acknowledgements

Thanks are due to Mary Eaton, and Deirdre, Bill and Barbara Baddeley, without whom this manuscript could not have been produced.

The authors and publishers would like to thank photographers Roy Pell and Alec Daniels for the sequence shots, Louis Ross and Peter Richardson for the use of their copyright photographs, and Fiona Elliott for her help in demonstrating for the sequences.

Badminton in Action

Steve Baddeley

with Richard Eaton

CANCELLED

WITHDRAWN AND SOLD

S
L   Johannesburg

Stanley Paul & Co. Ltd

An imprint of Century Hutchinson Ltd

62-65 Chandos Place, London WC2N 4NW

Century Hutchinson Australia (Pty) Ltd
88-91 Albion Street, Surrey Hills, NSW 2010

Century Hutchinson New Zealand Limited
PO Box 40-086, Glenfield, Auckland 10

Century Hutchinson South Africa (Pty) Ltd
PO Box 337, Bergvlei 2012, South Africa

First published 1988

© Steve Baddeley 1988

Set in Linotron Times

Design/typesetting by Roger Walker Graphic Design

Printed in Great Britain by
Butler & Tanner Ltd, Frome and London

ISBN 0 09 171320 X

This book is sold subject to the condition that it
shall not by way of trade or otherwise be lent,
resold, hired out or otherwise circulated without the
publisher's prior consent in any form of binding
other than that in which it is published and without
a similar condition including that condition being
imposed on the subsequent publisher

MANCHESTER
PUBLIC
LIBRARIES

88 821726

Preface

I shall never forget the day Steve Baddeley turned ten thousand people's emotions. That was in May 1984, in the giant saucer of the Stadium Negara in Kuala Lumpur – where degrees of heat competed with decibels of noise for possession of the senses, and where most of Malaysia expected sticky revenge to be enacted upon England for a Thomas Cup defeat two years previously.

Baddeley was first into the furnace. He was pitched in against Misbun Sidek, a man with a reputation for a dangerously devious wrist, outlandish hair styles, and frighteningly steep angles on his overheads. He was one of the world's top six players and had one of the world's most formidable crowds behind him.

Forty minutes later that crowd had turned from partisan support to booing dismissal of its man. Not that Misbun had disgraced himself. He had simply been beaten by an opponent with brains, bravery, and a big smash.

These are a long way from being Steve Baddeley's only assets, but he has used the three qualities more than any others to have contests played to his own strengths. By doing so on this memorable occasion he transformed the mood both of a match and of an entire Thomas Cup tie.
entire Thomas Cup tie.

The crowd continued to be critical after that, and Misbun was given a hard time again when he reappeared for the doubles. England went on to win 3–2. They also went on to win the bronze medal. It is the finest achievement they have ever managed, or are ever likely to. Baddeley's famous victory helped trigger it off.

Since then he has gone on to win the Commonwealth Games mens singles gold medal, taken two World Grand Prix titles, the Indian and the Scottish, finished third in the Grand Prix points table, and become the first Englishman since the war to reach the semi-finals of the All-England championships at Wembley. In the process he has developed into a man of many parts.

For instance, before winning the vital match that took him to the last four at Wembley, Steve interrupted his preparation to go through the nerve-racking experience of making a speech at a formal luncheon of officials and celebrities. He didn't have to, but he wanted to register his thanks for being given the Badminton Writers' annual award. For that he made many friends. Steve Baddeley may be successful but he is not selfish.

He has also been an occasional journalist, taken a keen interest in politics, been a leading light in the Players' Association and become one of badminton's best known personalities. Increasingly, too, he has become one of its best analysts. There could be few better with whom to attempt a book such as this.

Richard Eaton

The game

The movements of a shuttlecock are amongst the most pleasing sights in sport: flat and fast like the cone of a space capsule in orbit, then slowing and turning like a small parachute in a gravity-resistant eclipse as it descends to earth. The contrasts it creates are unique. Length, width, and height are all important in what is the most three-dimensional of all racket games. A slow-exposure photograph of a shuttlecock over the course of a few rallies would reveal the most ornate and intricate of patterns and parabolas, as though some hidden design of beauty lay behind it all.

Perhaps it does. There is an ancient mystery about the true origins of badminton. Versions of the game have been depicted on pottery that appeared around 3,000 years ago in China. There is evidence of it in Ancient Greece, and at about the same time in Japan, India, and Siam. There are medieval woodcuts of shuttles being hit with bats in England.

It is certain, however, that in English country houses during the mid-nineteenth century battledores were used to hit shuttles. Army

Sequence A:
Forehand smash

Sequence B:
Backhand clear

Sequence C:
Forehand
sliced drop

Sequence D:
High singles
serve

officers who learnt the game in India played it at Badminton Hall, on the Duke of Beaufort's country estate in Gloucestershire. From this, in 1869, badminton took its name.

Since then badminton's progress has been so steady that it has become a big sport in three continents and is continuing to make headway throughout the rest of the world. This is not surprising. The action of hitting a delicately feathered piece of cork is intrinsically pleasurable. The way in which it slows is both aesthetically pleasing, and enables the beginner to attain a degree of grace and dignity during those worrying early attempts.

This unique characteristic also makes for disguise and tactical complexities that are richly rewarding for the player who improves. Improvement to the highest level provides an intensely demanding test of stamina and skill and of brain, making it a form of physical chess.

These are the qualities that have attracted players and spectators in very large numbers. There are an estimated four million people playing in England, and 20,000 watched the World Championships in Beijing in 1987. Since going open in 1979 badminton has developed a lucrative World Grand Prix circuit, and the stimulus of being included in the Olympics in 1992 is enormous.

8

In a local sports or community centre you are almost certain to find badminton courts. Start with a friend, or ask someone to help you. It is wise to have a little coaching, both for immediate enjoyment and to improve your standard. The club or sports centre should help you obtain it.

The value of coaching is that it develops good habits. Many people stand still and hit to their opponent instead of seeking ways of making opponents move. It is important to take an overhead shot rather than hit it underarm, as many beginners do. For a good length or a powerful smash you need a sound technique and to make a mental photocopy of the shot so it can be reproduced. One very good way to do that is to look at the flicker sequences in this book.

But remember, many things work that cannot be found in this or any other coaching manual. We hope to reinforce the basics and help you find short cuts, but there is no one way to do things. The advice given here is, we believe, useful. But don't be a slave to it. Advice, knowledge, and technique are good servants but bad masters.

Equipment

Rackets

Since the early 1980's there has been a racket revolution, and wooden rackets have all but disappeared. There are, to date, three new types of racket: steel, aluminum, and graphite. (Graphite is sometimes mixed with compounds like Kevlar or Boron.) These materials are lighter, stronger, and faster through the air, so you can hit the shuttle harder and the rackets will last longer.

Choose the size of the handle of the racket carefully, according to what feels comfortable. The normal grip size is 3⅝ inches. The balance of rackets varies, so it will help your play if you become aware of the effects of head-heavy or head-light rackets. The better you get, the more you may want to experiment. There is a large choice of good-quality rackets, but it is not necessary to buy from the top end of the range to start with.

Strings

Good, tight stringing is important. Gut strings give more feel and sensitivity, but they are more expensive, so consider them only when you get to a reasonable standard. Meanwhile the feel of a really tight synthetic racket will compare quite favourably with gut. An increasing number of top players use synthetic strings because of their reliability and because they can be strung extremely tight.

Shuttles

Feather shuttles have a better 'feel' than plastic shuttles. This helps a player develop touch and control. But they cost twice as much as plastic, and will not last so long.

For a beginner plastic shuttles are adequate, but if you are good it is better to use feathers. Clubs vary; some use plastic, but many still use feathers.

Weights of shuttles vary a little and can be tested by striking them from the back of the court. They should land around the doubles service line. The rule says a shuttle is of the right pace when, hit by a player with a full underhand stroke, it falls not less than 1 ft. 9in. (530mm) and not more than 3 ft. 3in. (990mm) short of the other back boundary line.

Remember not to store feather shuttles near heat. The natural oils in the feathers can dry up, and then will break easily; so keep shuttles some-where cool, like a garage. A feather shuttle is a delicate piece of workman-ship – don't abuse it. Pick it up gently

11

from the floor; don't crush it by carelessly scooping it up.

Clothes

When choosing clothes, comfort is the main objective. There's nothing worse than a shirt that is tight under the armpits, or shorts that don't allow you to bend properly. Be certain that shorts feel comfortable in the lunging position and that your shirt does not restrict you in the overhead hitting position. Many women prefer to wear a skirt (or shorts) and a top, rather than a dress. Use padded socks to help avoid blisters.

Clothing can be prevented from becoming crumpled by using a racket-sized holdall. If you get a holdall, get a racket cover too: damp kit alongside a racket can damage the strings. A plastic bag is useful for damp kit and towels.

Shoes

There are a host of different badminton shoes these days. It is best if the soles have a good grip. Shock absorption is important, as badminton is a very physical game. Steve Baddeley Gold Badminton shoes have shock-absorbing material built into the soles. Whatever you buy, comfort is vital. And don't tie the laces too tightly, as this can cause bruising.

12

When you have finished playing, always keep warm. Wearing a track-suit is the best way to do this. It lessens the chances of aches and pains from stiffness.

Grips

Grips are made of leather, towelling, or synthetics. The advantage of towelling is that it can quickly be changed, and it gives a comfortable grip less likely to cause blisters. Leather is more expensive and difficult to change, but hard-wearing.

When you have your equipment, book a court at your local sports or community centre or club for half an hour. Don't overdo it to begin with by playing for too long.

13

How to hit (pronation and supination)

It is usually accepted that the first thing you have to learn is how to hold the racket. Well, we are going to be a little bit different. By first acquiring an awareness of how a shuttlecock is hit, the importance of learning the correct forehand grip can be better understood.

It is often said that badminton is a game where the wrist is important. In fact, the wrist has probably been over-rated. Biomechanical study of the overhead shots shows that the wrist actually plays only a minor role. The main source of power is an inward rotation of the upper arm on the forehand, called *pronation* of the forearm: and an outward rotation of the upper arm on the backhand, called *supination* of the forearm.

Don't be frightened off by the scientific-sounding terms. Crudely put, they mean that the forearm twists. This is more important than what you do with the wrist. It also means that if you get this right, you will get the grip right.

Pronation is simply the movement of the forearm turning from inside to out. It's a turning action of the

14

forearm in an anti-clockwise (right-hander), or clockwise (left-hander), direction. The palm ends up facing downwards.

Supination is twisting the other way, for the backhand. The rotation of the forearm is now clockwise for right-handers and anticlockwise for left-handers. Try doing shadow exercises with and without the racket.

Use the forearm properly, and there is a greater likelihood that you will adopt the correct grip.

Grips and stance

The advice in the following pages assumes the reader to be right-handed. If (like Steve Baddeley) you are left-handed, simply read right for left and vice versa. Some of the photographs do in fact show left-handed players.

Many beginners pick up the racket in a panhandle grip (see figure 1). The racket face is square to the body and the tendency is to hit with the wrist, which means there will be little power. The best you can manage is a short jabbing action.

To get power you need to pronate the forearm as described. Pick up the racket in the panhandle grip and pronate the forearm in a slow-motion overhead forehand. Can you see what will happen?

The racket face will strike the shuttle out to the right, whereas it needs to go in a straight line. So we need to establish a grip that allows the racket face to be square to the shuttle *after* the forearm has been pronated. This is the forehand grip.

Forehand grip

Here's how to find it. Hold the throat of the racket in the left hand with the racket head perpendicular to the floor.

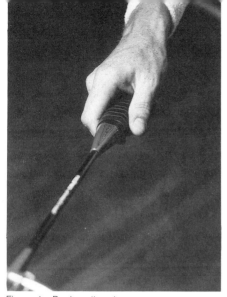

Figure 1   Panhandle grip

Place the palm of your racket hand flat on the strings. Slide it down and shake hands with the handle. The 'V' between the thumb and forefinger points roughly down the top bevel. Don't tense the hands or grip fiercely. It helps you spread your fingers slightly (see figure 2a).

Now try the forehand overhead again. To hit the shuttle straight you must pronate the forearm. If you don't, the shuttle will go sailing off to the left! If the forearm doesn't turn, the racket cannot connect square onto the shuttle

The importance of holding the racket lightly becomes obvious when you switch grips. You will sometimes need to switch when playing a backhand. Let's see how.

17

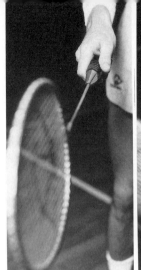 

Figure 2a Forehand grip   Figure 2b Backhand

Backhand grip

Holding the forehand grip, twist the racket slightly in a clockwise direction, using your non-racket hand. The racket turns in your right hand about one-eighth of the handle's circumference – until your thumb is resting along the flat part of the handle (see figure 2b).

Practise changing from one grip to the other, to become as quick and dextrous as possible. However, don't use the non-racket hand. It is only used as a teaching aid to discover the grips. After that, change grips with the fingers of the racket hand.

Panhandle grips

After all this, you can learn the panhandle grip. It can profitably be used around the net area, for kills and pushes, especially in doubles. The palm of the hand is more or less parallel to the flatter side of the handle – like holding a frying pan.

The size of the racket handle can also be important. Too small and it may make a player squeeze too tight. That can cause arm trouble. Usually the fingers will come round the handle so that they almost touch the palm.

Using the grips

Players at top level use a whole variety of grips. Some use an extreme forehand grip with more palm behind it for forehand shots, switching to the backhand where necessary. Others prefer a multi-purpose grip some-where closer to the backhand than the classic forearm grip. Then the grip change is minimal. It is vital *not* to use the panhandle for basic strokes or you will always be limited. The important point is to learn the relationship between the grip you are using and the angle of the racket face.

Stance

Between shots in a rally, the racket is best held in a relaxed forehand grip, not commited to either side, with the racket hand around waist height (see figure 3) of Zhao Jianhua. Many doubles players wait using the back-

Figure 3 Zhao Jianhua, the 1985 All England champion from China, in the ready position, with legs bent, eyes on the shuttle, racket just above waist height

hand grip when in a defensive position.

The racket head position should be variable. If you are expecting a smash or a downward shot, you are more likely to have the racket lower. If the opponent is struggling at the back of the court you will probably have it higher.

A player needs to be alert and ready to spring swiftly to any area. So the

20

knees need to be bent and the weight on the balls of the feet. The eyes should be fixed on the opponent, his racket, and the shuttle.

The base

Since in singles one needs to reach all areas, try to adopt a fairly central base position. That will be roughly 3 ft. behind the service line, along the middle line. It isn't fixed: different styles of players have different bases. Also, it will vary depending on what sort of player you are playing against and the state of the rally. If the shuttle is around the net area, the base has to be moved closer to the net. If a smash is expected, push the base back.

Try to avoid shots that will leave you unable to regain base – unless you are pretty certain of making a winner. Note that it is easier to move forward, but you may find you have less time because the shuttle will usually be coming down faster. It is harder to move backwards, but you have more time. So if you are central, that is about the right position for the base.

Finally, it is best to face the area of the court from where the shuttle will come. If an opponent is hitting from his or her deep backhand side, you should not stand square to the net but move to face at a slight angle, towards the shot that is coming.

21

Forehand overhead shots

It is worth looking in detail at the overhead forehand, because the technique is the same for clears, drops, and smashes. Get this right, and you probably have 40 per cent of the game right. Carefully shadow the following moves step by step. It will pay off.

Begin with a forehand grip in the relaxed but alert ready position. As the shuttle sails to the back of your court, move backwards with small, light, bouncing steps until you are behind it. Don't turn your back on the net as you do this. You can face forward and still maintain balance and rhythm as you move.

The preparation

The right hand is moved up close to the right shoulder. This brings the racket into the preparatory position. The racket head can be held at head height (see figure 4).

The last step must be with the right foot, so that it is further back in the court than the left foot. Then you are sideways to the net with the left shoulder leading. The left hand and arm point up towards the approaching shuttle. This improves balance and

Figure 4   Liem Swie King of Indonesia, three times All England champion, in a classic forehand overhead preparation position

helps to ensure that the upper body has turned sideways.

Preparation is now complete. This position can be held until you are ready to commence hitting. The sideways position can be established early in your backward movement from base but once it has been established, any further backward movements are better done with chassé movements (moving one foot up to, but not crossing over, the other).

23

Hitting

The racket starts the hitting motion by moving to a position behind the shoulders, or lower (see figure 5. Note also the forearm starting to turn). Cock the wrist as you lift the arm back. Once you have started the hitting motion, maintain a continous movement of the racket. Don't wait with the racket behind the head. Contact is made high above the head with an almost straight arm (see figure 7).

Figure 5 Morten Frost of Denmark, four times All England champion, doing a forehand overhead with the forearm starting to turn

Figure 6 Frost's overhead this time shows the forearm having turned and the full extension of the arm

Remember that the forearm must twist inwards (pronate) to develop maximum power and to hit the shuttle straight (see figure 6).

As the racket swings, the right foot begins to step forward. This ensures that the body weight is transferred forwards, giving more power. It also helps the recovery to the base position. Beginners often fail to step forwards and consequently have difficulty getting the shuttle to the other end of the court.

25

Figure 7 Sze Yu of Australia showing the importance of taking the shuttle high and early

Follow-through

The racket arm should go in the direction of the shuttle (see figure 8). Don't let the racket drop too low. The right foot completes its step and the left arm is pulled downwards and backwards past the body. The effect of the right-foot, left-arm movement is to complete the body rotation. The body will now once again be sideways to the net, but this time with the right shoulder leading.

After completing the stroke, the player should use short, light steps to regain the base position.

It is worth remembering that though we have divided this shot into three phases, this should not be reflected in the way you hit the shot. You don't want jerky motions like a puppet, but smooth, continuous, flowing movements.

Having mastered the rudiments of this technique it is then possible to look in more detail at the variety of overhead shots you can play. Plenty of interesting possibilities are now open to you! By hitting the shuttle in different overhead positions and with variable force you can play a wide variety of clears, drops and smashes. By using the same basic technique for each you can really keep the opponent guessing.

Figure 8 Jens-Peter Nierhoff of Denmark with his arm following through in the direction of the shuttle. There is a turn of forearm and wrist, to reverse slice the shuttle (see page 33). Compare with figure 5 where you see the heel of the wrist: here you see the back of the hand

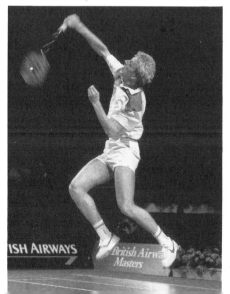

Clears

The high defensive clear

This is used to send the shuttle to the back of the opponent's court so that it drops straight down on to the back line.

To achieve this, contact with the shuttle is made slightly behind the head, or immediately above it. The technique of hitting is exactly as just described.

With the shuttle hit high into the air there is time to regain a balanced base position at a comfortable pace. It also makes it difficult for the opponent to play an attacking shot. There are two reasons for this:

1. You have made the opponent move to the rear of the court.
2. It is harder to smash a shuttle that is dropping straight down than one travelling flatter with the cork facing you.

The attacking clear

This has a flatter, faster path. Ideally, just above your opponent's outstretched racket. To create this, use the same technique as before, but make contact further forward than for the defensive

28

clear. This will usually be slightly forward of the head.

It is reckless to play the attacking clear if you are out of position. There is far less time than with the defensive clear to recover to base position. If the attacking clear is intercepted you could be left for dead. Played well, the shot will force the opponent back, and make him or her take the shuttle lower than (s)he would wish.

Drops

Slow drop

The aim of the slow drop is to make the shuttle fall in a steep arc so that it comes down as close to the net as possible.

The point of impact is similar to that of the defensive clear, but instead of following through, the hitting action is checked so that the shuttle is not struck too hard. However, it is important not to just dab at it: control is maintained by following through smoothly. If contact with the shuttle is made just behind the head it can be projected slightly upwards, facilitating its fall closer to the net.

However, be careful! The shuttle travels comparatively slowly, giving your opponent more time to reach it. Disguise or deception is therefore important. This is achieved by making absolutely sure the preparation is the same as for the clear.

Fast drop

The fast drop will travel further into court than the slow drop, landing between the front service line and the mid-court area.

With the same preparation as for the other strokes, the fast drop has an impact point just forward of the head. This sends the shuttle in a sharp downward direction. The racket-head speed must be slower at impact than for the clear (or smash) but need not be checked as for the slow drop.

With practice the fast drop can become very consistent. It need never drop close to the net, so the delicate touch required for the slow drop is not so necessary.

Sliced drop

This is a variation of the fast drop, with the racket head cutting across the base of the shuttle at an angle.

There are two major advantages:

1. The shuttle drops shorter, sometimes surprisingly shorter, than a shot hit flat, but the racket-head speed can be fast, suggesting a deeper shot; this is because power is lost on impact, due to the oblique contact.
2. The line of the follow-through of the racket will be different from that of the shuttle, creating deception.

Sometimes the racket-head speed is as fast as that of a smash, in which case the shot may be called a slice smash.

At an advanced level the vast majority of fast drops will be sliced,

31

Figure 9 Ib Frederiksen of Denmark, the 1988 All England champion, hits an overhead slice straight down the court

because they are much more deceptive than ordinary fast drops. There are two kinds:

Normal slice. The racket slices in a left-to-right direction. Make contact in front and just to the right of the body (see figure 9). The racket head continues towards the camera whilst the shuttle travels in a straight line. You can see the same shot played by a left hander in figure 10. The greater the slice, the less racket-head speed will be imparted to the shuttle, and the shorter it will fall. This is the most commonly used slice and is particular-

32

ly effective when struck from the forehand side across court. This enables it to be hit with a very fast action, yet still fall as short as the short-service line.

Reverse slice. The racket slices the shuttle in a right-to-left direction (see figure 11). It is usually played cross-court from the round-the-head position, with contact just to the left of the head. However, the impact point is rarely in front of the body, but above it, or even slightly behind it. Thus it is often hit with the back arching. The forearm must be twisted (pronated) for the racket to impart the glancing blow required.

Figure 10 Steve Baddeley hits an overhead forehand cross-court slice. Note the angle of the racket face that has sliced across the base of the shuttle

Figure 11 Fiona Elliott showing the impact of the reverse slice. The racket moves right to left

Smash

The aim of the smash is to hit down fast enough to beat the opponent or force a weak return. This is achieved by a fast racket-head at impact and by a flat contact. Slice will lead to loss of shuttle speed. Contact is made in front of the body, as for the fast drops.

Variation, pace and direction are all important. A steep smash hit accurately down either sideline is the classic ploy and will reach the floor quickest. Try smashing cross-court or straight at the opponent, or hit a flatter smash into the back tramlines.

At a high level it is possible to use a jump smash, popularised by the Far Eastern players. Many of them become airborne before smashing, thus gaining steepness in the trajectory (see figures 12 and 13). However, it is a very tiring shot, and recovery takes longer.

Use of overheads

There is a kind of built-in deception when clear, drop, and smash all look identical and the opponent doesn't know what's coming. But you can also develop a more deliberate deception: for example, exaggerating the power

34

Figure 12 Yang Yang of China, the 1987
World champion, taking the shuttle early

and tension of the body as though a
smash is coming, but producing a drop
instead.

Although we have put all these shots
into different categories, in reality
they exist in a continuum. For
example, there are many different
types of clear between the high
defensive clear and the attacking clear.
Nor is there any definite spot where a
fast drop becomes a smash.

35

Figure 13 Zhao Jianhua getting really high with his spectacular jump smash

Remember, too, that the impact points suggested are only guides. They will vary from player to player and situation to situation.

When you have achieved a basic level of ability, experiment with a variety of shots. Learn to understand the interrelationship between body position, shuttle position, and racket-head speed and direction. These factors can be juggled to create a profusion of strokes.

36

Round-the-head shots

When the opponent hits the shuttle to the backhand rear corner, you can play a backhand or try to move quickly and play a forehand. Usually players try for the latter option. Sometimes the shuttle can be struck directly overhead, but often it is taken to the left of the body (or to the right for a left hander). When it is, we can easily see why it is called a round-the-head shot (see figure 14).

Figure 14 Steve Baddeley playing a round-the-head clear from the backhand corner. Note the position the shuttle is hit in relation to the body

Such a movement is more tiring than playing a backhand, but it greatly increases power and potential deception. It also enables a reverse slice drop to be played very effectively.

Movement

Move from the base towards the round-the-head corner and establish a sideways position with the left foot in front of the right. As you make the last step, push off with a backward jump, hitting the shuttle in mid-air. During the stroke the left foot kicks backward and the right foot forward, so that the left foot lands further back than the right foot (see figure 15). You have

Figure 15 Icuk Sugiarto of Indonesia, the 1983 World champion, doing a scissor kick whilst executing a round-the-head shot

Figure 16 Helen Troke, European champion in 1984 and 1986, does a powerful scissor kick during a reverse slice drop

transferred your weight as in a normal forehand stroke – but in mid air (see figure 16)! This is called a 'scissor-kick'. It is a difficult movement because the whole shot has to be well timed right from early on in the movement.

Round-the-head shots can also be played by moving back to a position behind the shuttle and playing the shot in the normal way, with the right foot stepping forward. As this happens, the body leans to the left. The upper body will normally stay fairly square on to the net during the preparation.

The most natural round-the-head shots tend to be the cross-court reversed slice drops (fast or slow), the straight clear, and the straight smash, which is often extremely powerful.

39

Overhead backhand shots

No matter how valuable round-the-head shots may prove, don't neglect the backhand. There will always be times when it will be exposed.

Pointers

Backhands can cause problems for players at all levels. It is worth making a few points clear before looking at technique:

1. An overhead backhand requires good timing and technique – not strength.
2. The backhand clear is an *impact* shot: the follow-through is checked.
3. Do *not* point the elbow up at the the shuttle as you prepare.
4. Unlike the forehand there is *no* weight transference. You should be able to play a backhand on one leg or standing on a chair. You shouldn't fall off!

Hitting action

The right foot steps over the left foot towards the rear of the court, so you have your back to the net. It is not necessary to use the backhand grip. However, the thumb behind the

Figure 17 Paul-Erik Hoyer of Denmark reaching to take an early, high overhead backhand

handle on a backhand grip can be an aid for guiding the shuttle. What is essential is to learn the relationship between the grip and the angle of the racket face.

Have the elbow tucked into the body. As the stroke begins, the elbow and upper arm move upwards towards the shuttle. At this point the arm straightens, the forearm twists (supination), and contact is made as high as possible (see figure 17).

41

Figure 18 Darren Hall, European champion in 1988, has little follow-through on his backhand

There is no real follow-through, as you can see in figure 18, where Darren Hall's backhand is lower than Hoyer's. Do not try to transfer body weight into the shot. The right foot makes contact with the floor as you make contact with the shuttle.

By tucking your elbow into your body during preparation, you keep your racket around waist height or lower. This gives a longer build-up, compared with the common fault of pointing the elbow up to the shuttle, and enables you to generate racket-head speed, thus imparting power. You need to be very strong indeed to achieve sufficient power if you start with your elbow up and the racket high.

Think about the forehand stroke. If you start with the racket behind your head and your elbow pointing to the shuttle, you won't be able to generate as much power as with a full stroke. It is the same on the backhand. Starting with the elbow up means you are starting half-way through the stroke.

Drop shot

To gain deception, the preparation for the drop shot must be identical to that for the clear. At the last moment the racket-head speed is checked so that the shuttle is not hit too hard. Control is gained by following through smoothly, as with the forehand drop.

Continue the follow-through movement and use this to commence the recovery to base.

A word of warning: the backhand overhead drop should be hit fairly fast because opponents will be looking for a weak return. Too slow a drop may enable an enterprising opponent to come in and play a kill.

At an advanced level, the backhand drop is hit by 'cutting' round the

43

outside of the shuttle, contacting both base and skirt and thus gaining greater control.

The smash

Using the same technique as for the clear. Strike the shuttle in a downward direction by bringing the wrist right over at impact. The follow-through is checked. Don't worry too much about this shot, as even very good players find it difficult.

The Danish Swipe

This is not a shot to be advocated, but it can get you out of trouble as a kind of drive-cum-clear when the shuttle is in the backhand corner. It is some-times effective for club players who cannot play the overhead backhand.

It is played by moving towards the backhand corner and waiting for the shuttle to drop below shoulder height. Move the right foot into the shuttle, point the elbow, and sweep the arm into the shot, following through strongly. It is quite a powerful shot: the body goes forward and there is quite a bit of swinging forward and twisting into it. Hit it hard and high, so that there is a chance of recovering a reasonable position, or drive it fast and flat to pressurise the opponent. If you find it effective, use it in matches and practise the overhead technique at other times.

Net shots

Many matches are won and lost at the net. In singles an opponent can be tied up at the net and frustrated. Baddeley's best battles have often been won that way! The essence of creative net shots is delicacy and touch, and in winning net shots, speed and anticipation.

Movement

There are three main ways of moving from the base to the net – two types of stepping and a chassé. All end with a lunge to get to the net quickly whilst on balance.

One of the stepping movements makes the left foot go behind the leading foot; the other has it going in front of the leading foot. The chassé is done by drawing the left foot up to the right, which continues the movement in the same direction. The final step, or lunge, often covers a great deal of court in one step.

Use any of these for moving from base to the net. It is vital that the final step, the lunge, is with the *right* foot (see figure 19).

Another essential is to take the shuttle as high as possible, ideally at

45

46

tape height. (If you meet the shuttle higher than that you will probably be attempting a kill.) The arm will be outstretched and the racket should move in the simplest possible line from the body. Look at figures 20 and 21. In figure 20 Steve Baddeley has taken the shuttle early and high; in figure 21 Michael Kjeldsen has made the shuttle start to turn. Both are well balanced and have lunged with the racket leg.

◄ Figure 19   Darren Hall moves swiftly, lunging on his racket leg to play a backhand with a backhand grip

Figure 20   Steve Baddeley takes a high early net shot against Morten Frost

47

Figure 21   Michael Kjeldsen, the 1988 Danish national champion, playing a net shot off the racket leg with a backhand grip. He has made the shuttle turn before it goes over the net

Hitting

The principles are the same on both backhand and forehand. A net shot requires a very short backswing and follow-through. It is a very delicate, gentle stroke. Because you don't need power, grips can vary. Don't let the shuttle passively bounce off the strings. Caress it over, close to the tape.

When players start, they sometimes jab at the shuttle from below. Try to avoid this by developing a delicate touch. There is a great contrast: you come in very powerfully and then need

48

to be using a gentle touch. It's all done together – so it is a testing combination to achieve. That is one of the beauties of badminton.

Delicacy is aided by a light grip, as it is a combined movement of hand, wrist, and fingers that produces the control. You can make very large and rapid improvements in your touch and control through practice.

It is important with net shots to experiment, and there is plenty of scope for individualism. Remember: in singles the vital but difficult thing is to get to the shuttle early. The earlier you reach the shuttle, the easier it is to play an effective net shot.

Net shots can be played without deception, when a player gets there quickly and plays it over, believing he has reached it early enough not to be threatened. More often, however, you will want to suggest an alternative shot. That usually means threatening a flick shot over your opponent's head (see page 53).

Spins

As you meet the base of the shuttle it is simple to impart a slight spin, or turn, with a brushing action (see figure 21). Using your wrist, cut across the base, in either direction. It is easier from right to left on the forehand, and from left to right on the backhand. The idea is to make the shuttle turn

49

over, so that as it crosses the net the cork will not always be presented to the opponent's racket. If he tries to hit the feathers he will have very little control.

Hairpins

If the shuttle has dropped very low, spins are usually too hazardous. Instead it has to be returned in a trajectory that forms a hairpin. The shuttle crosses the net and descends very steeply the other side. This shot requires delicacy of touch, as it must lose pace and start to come down just above tape height.

Kills

If you take the shuttle above the tape, hit it down and try to make a winning shot. Do not follow through, or you may hit the net. It is an impact shot.

Move as you would to the other net shots, although a little more explosively to get the shuttle slightly higher.

On the forehand side use the normal forehand grip, or the panhandle grip if you prefer. On the backhand you need the classic backhand grip, with the thumb down the back (see figure 22). Don't follow through because, as well as the risk of hitting the net, there is a need to have the racket up ready for the reply. The racket will move from the ready position around the waist and, as you come in, move it up and

50

Figure 22 Jan-Eric Antonsson of Sweden trying a backhand kill. Note the grip with the thumb behind the handle

back to around head height. Do not use a big swing, just a controlled one.

From head height bring the racket forward with a short movement. On the backhand side, the forearm will twist (supinate). On the forehand it is more of a dab, especially if it is played with the panhandle grip. Keep the head, chest, and body up, so that there

Figure 23   Sze Yu about to play a forehand kill

is no tendency to collapse with the shot (see figure 23). Most likely you will play the shot either before your right foot lands, or as it lands. After landing, get your racket head up again and be ready to recover.

From the net: flick and high lift

The flick

If you learn the flick as an alternative to a net shot, you will have the options of playing the shuttle delicately over the net, or flicking it with a fast, short action to the back.

It helps to be aware with peripheral vision of what the opponent is doing. If you see him moving in, then flick the shuttle to the back. As you approach the net, it is best to have the wrist held back, or cocked, so you can threaten either a flick or a net shot.

On the backhand side you need to come in with the backhand grip (see figure 25). It is relatively easy to flick to the back of the court, although you will need to use the backhand grip on the backhand side. There will be forearm twist in conjunction with the wrist (see figure 24).

You won't always want to flick it high. Sometimes you can flick flat and fast down the side of the court, particularly if your opponent is moving in for the net shot.

High lift

There is an important distinction between the flick and the high lift.

Figure 24   Morten Frost doing a forehand flick against Icuk Sugiarto

Whereas the flick is a threatening shot, the high lift from the net is defensive, particularly when played from half-way down the net or lower. From this position a net shot is still possible, but a flick is difficult because of the lack of

angle to play with. When you take it very low you will need quite a lot of power to get the shuttle to the back. This can only be achieved with a larger swing.

The actions of the lift and the flick

Figure 25   Steve Baddeley plays a backhand flick over Jens-Peter Nierhoff

may be similar but the effect is different. When the lift goes high it should drop straight down at the back of the court. The flick goes flatter and faster, in more of a parabola.

With the high lift you can extend the backswing to generate more racket-head speed. It doesn't really matter that you telegraph your intentions, because the shuttle should go too high to be cut off. The final part of the shot will be the same as for the flick: a forearm twist on the backhand, and the use of the wrist on the forehand.

As before, use the backhand grip for the backhand and the forehand grip for the forehand. For both backhand and forehand you *must* come in on the right leg. If you don't, you will lose distance and balance.

Remember, too, that there should be adequate recovery time after the high lift, but with the flick you can be vulnerable. If your opponent reads it and intercepts it you can be caught out of position. That is in the nature of any fast attacking shot. So think about when to flick and when to lift.

Defence

Plenty of good players base their game on defence and are happiest when the opponent is smashing. They like the shuttle to be hit fast at them, because that may enable them to get their opponent out of position. Defence can create an opportunity to attack.

Even if we do not categorise Morten Frost as a defensive player – perhaps he bases his game more on speed – there are many top players who are. The 1985 World Champion, Han Jian, certainly was and so is Icuk Sugiarto, the 1983 World Champion, and Nick Yates, the experienced England international.

Defence should be used both to return the shuttle safely and to attack. First, however, learn to return the smash safely.

Movement

On the forehand all defensive shots are played off the right foot, which will need to be pushed rapidly out towards the sideline. Often one step will be adequate, but you may need a shuffle or chassé first to reach very wide shots. Left handers move the left leg.

57

Figure 26   Helen Troke shows poise and balance as she hurries to return a drop to the forehand

Figure 27   Prakash Padukone, the 1980 All England champion, plays a backhand defence off his left foot. Compare this with Nick Yates' step over defence in figure 28

Figure 28 Nick Yates retrieves a smash wide to his backhand by stepping across with his right foot. Compare this with Prakash Padukone's footwork in figure 27

On the backhand, lunge across where possible with the left foot, and make the return off this leg (see figure 27). However, it is not possible to reach a wide smash in this way. The racket comes across the body, and cannot reach so far. It will be necessary therefore to take a small sideways step with the left foot and then lunge across with the right (see figure 28). The return will be made off the right leg. Recovery is slower from this position, so only use the 'step-over' when really necessary.

To defend against smashes directed at the body, there are two methods.

Figure 29 Razif Sidek of Malaysia defending, taking the shuttle off his right hip and in front of him. He and his watching brother Jalani won the 1982 All England mens doubles title

Figure 30 Morten Frost, on base, perfectly balanced, defending with a forehand block against a smash

Take the shuttle in front of the body (see figure 29), or move the body out of the way. The latter requires nimble footwork, so that space is created in which to play the return. Usually there is only time to use the first method.

To react quickly enough to return a smash, a good base position and good ready position are vital (see section on grips and stance). The base position should be flexible. The stronger the

attack, the further back you may want to be. Usually it is best to have the racket in front of the body, ready to move to either side.

You often see good players anticipating which side the smash is directed. That is because 'telegraphing' the smash – sending inadvertent messages about where it is going – is common. Anticipate, by all means. But remember: if this policy succeeds

61

once, and you make a penetrating return off your opponent's smash, (s)he may adjust this shot next time.

Block

The block is the defensive shot to learn first. The shuttle is played back to the opponent's front court. From a very powerful smash you may only have time for the shuttle to bounce off the racket over the net. However, when possible try to use a short backswing, as this is more deceptive.

Learn to block straight, then cross-court. The cross-court block makes it tough for the smasher because (s)he has to go from the back corner to the opposite front corner, the furthest movement. You can either guide the follow-through to caress the shuttle over the net, or impact the shuttle using the angle of the racket face to create the trajectory. By combining these factors, two types of block can be played.

One is a *hairpin block*. This is hit slightly upwards, so as to drop close to the net, and perpendicular to it, like a slow drop. The other is a *flat block*, played flatter and faster, to cross just above net height, deeper into the opponent's court.

The advantage of the hairpin is that it brings the opponent right into the net. Its disadvantages are that it is a slower shot – giving the opponent

62

more time to react – and it is harder to play well. If the opponent does reach it early he may kill it or play a tight net shot.

The advantage of the flat block is that, as a faster shot, it is harder for an opponent to reply with a tight net shot. A disadvantage is that it is easier for him to reach. At international level the very tight block would only be employed against a tired opponent, or perhaps one who has smashed off-balance.

Lift

The aim of the defensive lift is to return the shuttle to the rear of the court. It is important to ensure that it goes high over the opponent's racket, otherwise it may present an easy opportunity to smash.

The more backswing you can use, the better chance of lifting to a length. It can be difficult to lift to a good length against a powerful smash as there is only a short time to generate racket-head speed. The backhand is aided by guidance from the thumb, so, if there is time, getting the racket round into the backhand grip is valuable.

Try to follow through smoothly. Those with a strong wrist, and forearm, a good hitting action, and good timing will certainly lift to a length without difficulty.Even if you

find it difficult, try not to tense up. That may cause the forearm and wrist to lock, reducing both control and power.

Flick

This is faster and flatter than the lift and although played in a similar way, the angle is different. Usually it is an impact shot with a limited follow-through. Timing is everything; you need to use the power of the smash to your advantage.

Aim to return the shuttle swiftly to the rear court while the opponent is struggling to recover from completing a smash. It is risky because it can be intercepted, but it may tempt him to move very fast to intercept, thus tiring him. The speed of the return may also elicit an error.

Off a straight smash, the flick is nearly always played across court, into the open space. At best, the flick can be devastating, leaving the opponent scrambling in a back corner.

With all defensive shots relaxation is important. At club level quite a lot of players are leaden-footed, and tense in the arm. If you stay relaxed and alert even the best smashes can be returned.

Singles service

The demands of the law on serving are so stringent that the server usually starts off at a disadvantage. This has been so marked in doubles that it has led to an ongoing debate about whether or not to change the rules.

The receiver's advantage is less clear-cut in singles. He has a longer court to cover, and should be more wary about committing himself to a return that leaves him out of position.

High serve

The aim of the high serve is to move the opponent as far back as possible, making it hard to start an attack. Because it moves him the maximum distance, he will be left out of position if he tries a fast attacking shot.

As well as achieving a good length it is advantageous to hit the shuttle high. This makes it drop almost straight, which is far harder to attack.

Stand 1-3 feet from the front line, and close to the middle line. Use the forehand grip for a high serve and (assuming you are a right-hander) put the left foot forward about 18 inches. This will aid comfortable balance.

65

Face towards the diagonally opposite service court and hold the shuttle by the top of the feathers, with the feathers upwards. If it were allowed to drop, it would land 12 inches to the right of the leading foot, level with the toes. Let the shuttle fall a couple of feet, and strike it just above knee height. The front knee should be relaxed, not stiff; otherwise it tends to lock the buttocks and the back.

The wrist, slightly cocked, is above the elbow as the arm is taken back. When it sweeps down there is a releasing of the wrist just before impact, and, as it becomes an extension of the arm, it locks. There should be a solid feeling when the high serve is struck, and the whole action should be smooth and flowing.

As the shuttle is struck, the body weight comes forward, and there is a slight twisting of the trunk, but the head stays level. The follow-through should be long and high to give the shuttle height and depth. There is plenty of time to establish base position.

A slight transfer of weight during the high serve gives extra power and rhythm. This transfer can be seen in the feet: often the front foot will start with only the heel touching the court. On completion of the shot the back foot is on the toes.

Aim for the middle of the back line of the service court. There are advantages in serving wide or straight but the risk of error is greater, and to miss a serve in singles is a crime! Depth and height are more important than position along the back line.

Low serve

No matter how good the high serve is, the chances are that it will give the initiative to the opponent. The low service has therefore gained in popularity since the mid-seventies. Now many leading men serve low, some as much as 90 per cent of the time. In women's singles, however, the high serve still dominates.

Take full advantage of the rules, and get the racket well above the knees when you make contact. Relax. You need an action that is very consistent, so that it can be performed under pressure. It should also enable you to flick, to stop opponents anticipating. Therefore try to hold the wrist back, keeping it cocked as long as possible. Stay well balanced, don't have too short a preparatory swing, and follow through smoothly. It is neither practical nor necessary to have the same build-up for both the high and the low serve. It does not matter if you telegraph the high serve: the opponent has plenty of time to see it anyway.

67

The low serve should pass close to the net tape, but don't make mistakes by playing it too tight. In singles, only an opponent of the highest standard will kill the return. Variation, however, is important, and this can be brought about by serving to different positions along the front line, and to different depths.

Flick serve

This should be hit in a flat arc, just high enough so that your opponent cannot reach it, but dropping after it has gone past him. It stops the opponent rushing in fast on the low service, and should have the same technique as the low service, except that the wrist is uncocked at the last moment.

It is illegal to use two actions in the same serve, so it will be unusual for the flick serve to be deceptive enough to be an outright winner. However, a good flick will force opponents to take the shuttle behind them.

Be careful, because a bad flick or an anticipated flick can give the receiver a simple half-court smash. Therefore it *must* have the same preparation as the low serve.

Backhand serve

This is not a common variation, but it is used by some of the best Indonesians, particularly Icuk Sugiarto. The main disadvantage with it is that it is difficult to serve a good-length flick with the backhand, which allows the receiver to move up the court to meet the low serve early.

Drive serve

A drive serve is hit fast and flat, often to head height. This can rush the receiver and cause an error. It may also entice the receiver to attack, but usually (s)he will smash back along the same path, which can be anticipated. However, there is quite a large element of risk in using this serve, as a good smash return can sometimes result.

The most effective drive serve is usually done by standing slightly wider than usual in the right-hand court, and driving down the receiver's backhand towards the back centre line. This often leads to a smash back to the server's forehand, which can be anticipated. Beware of the agile opponent who may be able to smash into the open gap left down the server's backhand.

Remember: the essence of good serving is variety. A high serve can go to different altitudes. A low serve can be pushed further and faster so that it doesn't hang over the net. Vary the trajectory, the direction, and the speed. Use all the different serves in varying combinations.

Singles tactics

It is obvious that you should play to opponents' weaknesses and avoid their strengths. For example, some players are very deceptive around the net: consequently, serving high to them would be a sensible initial tactic. If such an opponent serves low to you, then a deep lift or a flat push to the corners would be the best reply.

Many of your opponents will have weak overhead backhands. To expose this weakness, it is not sufficient just to clear or lift to the backhand corner, as this would usually result in a round-the-head reply. You need to move your opponent out of position – probably drawing them into the front forehand corner – and then play to the rear backhand side so that they have to play a backhand.

A weakness is often considered to be the area in which players make most mistakes. However, it is also worth noticing from where they make least winners. Commonly this is the rear forehand corner. When in trouble, this will often be a safe place to which to hit (see figure 31, where the best that Steve Baddeley can do is play

Figure 31   Steve Baddeley takes a shuttle in a difficult position, low in the forehand corner.

to a safe place and thrust back to base as fast as possible).

Think, too, of the overall type of game. Some players like a fast, flat game, full of smashes, fast drops and net play. Others prefer a slower, more controlled game, using the full length and width of the court, with high clears and slow drops. Some like to defend, using the power of the smash by

71

changing its direction and making the attacker work hard to recover from his shot.

What do you do if your best style of play suits the opponent's best style? The answer will vary from situation to situation, but where possible it is probably better to play your natural game. It is hard to play in an unfamiliar style when under pressure. However, lack of adaptability can lose you matches.

Sequences

With experience you will learn that patterns, or sequences, of shots are often repeated many times in matches. This is often because a shot is so effective that it forces the opponent to play a specific return. An excellent example of this often occurs when a steep, powerful smash is played close to the sidelines. This can leave the defender time only to get the racket into the path of the shuttle, and this limits the return to a straight block. By anticipating this reply, the attacker can move quickly in towards the net and take the shuttle early, killing the shuttle, or playing an effective spin net shot.

Another example of this idea is as follows. Play a fast clear into your opponent's forehand corner. If you are able to cause the shuttle to be taken from behind or with a bent arm from

72

head height or below (see figure 31), then the usual return, by most players, will be a straight drop. You can anticipate this and gain a commanding position in the rally.

How can you prevent the same thing happening to you? Quite simply, you must learn to play *at least* two shots from any position on the court. This will help to prevent your opponent from anticipating too early the shot you are about to play.

Imagine you are caught playing the shuttle from deep in your backhand or forehand corners. You may be unable to hit a good clear from this situation, especially on the backhand. The easiest return is a straight drop (as mentioned above), but you should develop a cross-court drop as well. This doesn't have to be played too often – you simply have to let your opponent know that you are capable of an alternative shot, so that the return cannot be foreseen. You may also be able to develop a powerful drive, using a Danish swipe on the backhand or a kind of squash shot on the forehand.

Cross-court shots

All the shots we have discussed can be hit straight or cross-court. There are several disadvantages of playing cross-court: the shuttle travels further and so gives the opponent more time to react,

73

the striker is left further out of position, and the shuttle passes across the central line and is prone to being intercepted.

However, cross-court shots do have the advantage of making opponents turn, a major weakness in many players. Sometimes players will establish a position on the base which faces the shuttle but closes the body slightly to a cross-court, so accentuating the turn they have to make to retrieve a cross-court shot. Cut drops are particularly effective cross-court as they can be played at a steeper angle and so drop closer to the net than a straight cut drop.

Margin of error

Singles is a game of many factors, two of which to some extent are opposed: consistency and accuracy. When considering this opposition we have to think about margin of error. For instance, when hitting a drop or a smash it is silly to aim for the lines, as this will usually result in a large number of errors. Work out your own margin. If you can smash within a foot of a given spot consistently, then aim it to go a foot inside the sideline. Then your most wayward shot may still land in.

This applies to all shots, though sometimes it will be necessary to take risks to win points.

Doubles

The doubles game is hugely popular in Britain, and represents many people's experience of badminton. As well as being an extremely sociable way of playing, it is full of variety and entertainment, both in its strokes and its tactics.

The basic techniques on overheads, defence, and net shots are the same for doubles. However, the placements, the frequency of use of each shot, and the tactics are very different. There are two basic formations in doubles: the attacking, in which players adopt front and back positions, and the defending, in which players are roughly side by side (see figure 32). Generally when one partnership is in one of these formations, their opponents should be using the other one.

Men's doubles

Generally speaking, it is better to attack, as you will be controlling the game. The attacking pair can hit down whilst the defensive pair are forced to lift. Park Joo Bong and Kim Moon Soo of South Korea, the 1985 World Champions, and Li Yongbo and Tian Bingyi of China, the 1987 World

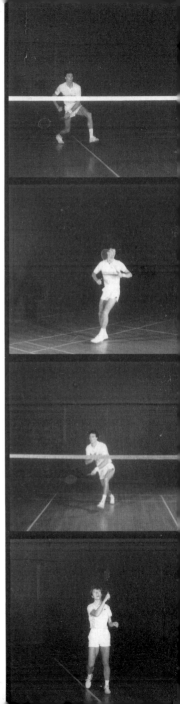

Figure 32 Attacking and defensive positions in doubles, with Shuuji Matsuno and Shinji Matsuura of Japan attacking against Michael Kjeldsen and Jens-Peter Nierhoff of Denmark

Champions, are both primarily attacking combinations.

Women's doubles

Women at international level have reactions comparable to men's, and so can defend almost as well as men. However, women do not smash so hard, and thus defence can dominate play at the highest level. This is especially noticeable with the Chinese and South Korean pairs, resulting in long rallies with little incentive for either pair to attack.

However, this is a recent development; Nora Perry and Jane Webster won the 1980 World Championship by attack, and at club and county level an attacking game can still reign supreme.

Serve

Look at the position of the server and the partner in figure 33. The serve should be aimed low, gaining the attack by forcing the opponent to lift.

There are many styles of serving, but you always need to be balanced and to stand close to the 'T'. Too far back and you leave a gap in the forecourt.

Make use of the limits of the laws by making contact with the shuttle as high as legally possible. This can be achieved by bending the arm at the elbow, shortening the grip, making contact with the shuttle out to the side of the body, or by combining these factors.

It is important to have a consistent, smooth action that can be repeated under pressure. Therefore keep it simple. The action is just a little push.

77

Figure 33   Billy Gilliland and Dan Travers, 1986 Commonwealth Gold medallists, in doubles serving positions. Gilliland toes the line whilst serving well out in front of the body. Travers has his racket up and legs bent

A slight rocking forward of the body may help to generate smoothness and rhythm.

The placement of the shuttle can be made to any point along the front line. Common targets are to the 'T', and wide, but use the space in between as well. Serve to the receiver's weakest spot: for example, the backhand if the opponent prefers the forehand.

The shuttle should pass over the net as close to the tape as possible. The highest point of its flight should be as it crosses the tape, so that it dips downwards into the opponent's court.

Vary the depth. Usually it should land on the front line, but sometimes push it a foot or two into the service box. Also vary the position from which you serve: moving just a few inches away from the middle line can unsettle your opponent by altering the angle of flight.

After the service is complete lift the racket to head height, incorporating this in the follow through. This enables you to be ready for a return to the net, and intimidates the opponent. Also, make as part of the follow-through a movement towards the net.

Backhand serve

The backhand serve should be struck further in front of the body than the

forehand (see figure 33). Use the backhand grip, which provides enough power to create a variation of the flick serve. Many people find the backhand an easier serve. There is a half-uncocking of the wrist, and the position of the hand usually makes this a comfortable and natural movement. By keeping the elbow up, it is easy to contact the shuttle high. Striking the shuttle from the hand reduces the margin of error. You can strike the shuttle close to the net by 'toeing the line' and leaning forward. This cuts down the reaction time for the receiver. Since the service action is so simple, many players find it quite easy to develop a consistent backhand serve.

However, the backhand serve does have disadvantages. It takes marginally longer to get the racket up after the serve, and you need to change to a forehand grip to prepare for the third shot. Also, it is harder to vary the direction of serve along the front line and it is more difficult to develop a good length flick.

The flick

This serve is hit towards the rear of the receiver's court. It should travel in a fast, flat arc but still out of the opponent's reach.

It is important that the preparation for the flick and low serve is identical, uncocking the wrist at the last moment to produce the flick. Make sure the trajectory goes over the opponent. If (s)he cuts it out, it may present an easy smash.

Return of serve

Look at the serving and receiving positions in figure 34. The return of serve requires great concentration and alertness (see figure 35). It also requires skill and knowledge. There are four main types of return in doubles:

(a) To the net

When this is played straight it is often the easiest way of getting a lift. Hitting the return to the sides is more difficult, but is a useful variation.

(b) At the opponents

1. A delicate push can hit the server in the chest as (s)he moves forward. If allowed to land it would fall just beyond the 'T'. It is useful against servers who quickly follow their serve to try to prevent you playing to the net.

2. A harder push at the chest of the server's partner is effective, but be careful not to push the shuttle out the back.

81

Figure 34 1988 World doubles champions Tian Bingyi and Li Yongbo of China, and Eddie Hartono and Sutanto Hadibowo of Indonesia, in the classic return of serve and serving positions

Figure 35 A study in concentration whilst receiving serve: Gillian Gowers and Gill Clark, the 1986 European womens doubles champions

(c) To the mid-court

A push down either sideline often finds a gap in the mid-court between the opponents.

(d) To the rear-court

1. A flat push to either corner is effective if both opponents are moving up the court to crowd the return.

2. A lift to the corners, which may be negative, but is sometimes necessary – especially if you have started to leave the serve, thinking it may land short.

83

Tactics

When returning a serve, try and take it early. Hustle a low serve. This is necessary because generally speaking it is important to attack. For the same reason the net player must always be alert, with the racket up, ready to take the shuttle early. If your side has the attack, the player in the rear-court should hit downwards with smashes or drops, trying to create opportunities for the net player to hit winners (see figure 36).

Smash

Vary the power, steepness, and placement of the smash. Usually you should smash to the straight player, and best of all at the chest, the inner hip (i.e. on the racket side), or the point where the opponent changes from forehand to backhand. Smashing straight helps your partner, facing forward at the net, to know where the shuttle will be hit to. The net player can then watch the straight defender and move over slightly to that side of the court. If you hit cross-court, you effectively cut your partner out at the net and also open up your own court.

Be wary of smashing down the tramlines even if there appears to be a gap. It is better to aim between your opponents, where both may go for it, or, even better, leave it.

Figure 36   Bingyi and Yongbo in the attacking doubles formation. Bingyi is doing a jump smash; Yongbo is alert in the forecourt

Slow drop

Use this and the cut drop as variations. Slow drops should go to the middle or straight, but rarely cross-court. If deceptive and used in combination with the smash they can be extremely effective. Li Yongbo, World Doubles Champion in 1987, does it well. Body deception (plus a loud grunt!) can suggest a big smash, and the drop comes at the last moment.

Defensive formation

The basic defence formation is side by side in the mid-court area.

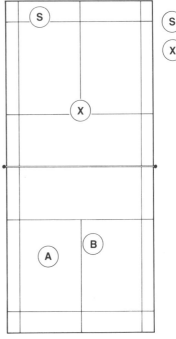

S) smasher

X) smasher's partner

In the diagram the shuttle is about to be smashed from the attackers' forehand court. Defender 'A' is ready to receive a straight smash. Defender 'B' can afford to move towards the centre and slightly closer to the net. 'A' takes smashes down the line and around the body. 'B' covers all smashes to the right of 'A'. This is a general rule and partners need to learn exactly where they expect each others' responsibilities to start and finish, especially with shots between them. A near image of this is in figure 37. A variation on defence that can be useful in doubles is the crouch defence (see figure 38).

The drive

The drive is used much more frequently in doubles than in singles and is played when the shuttle has dropped too low to make contact overhead. It is usually played in the half-court or back-court area and hit from about chest height to pass close to the tape; it can either land deep in the opposing court, or be hit more gently into the opposition's mid-court area.

To produce the shot, whether on the backhand or the forehand, the right foot should step out towards the sideline. On the backhand side it is best to employ a backhand grip. The shoulders turn, the wrist is cocked, and the racket is thrown at the shuttle. Take it at its maximum height and at arm's length, slightly in front of the body. Lean towards the shuttle, and follow through across your chest. You should be able to recover quickly, pushing off the right foot.

Mixed doubles

In mixed doubles the man is usually stronger than the woman and there-

88

Figure 37 Defensive doubles positions from Hartono and Hadibowo, attacking from Bingyi and Yongbo. Note the geometry, with all four players moving towards one side and the shuttle having just crossed the net from the backhand corner

Figure 38 Liem Swie King playing the crouch defence, partnered by Eddie Hartono

fore plays at the back, with the woman at the net. Suitable tactics are developed directly from this. Try to get the opposing woman to the back, where she may find it hard to kill the shuttle. To achieve this you can serve low to the man to draw him forward, and high to the woman. It may be worth taking a wide position on the forehand side when serving, and driving it down the woman's backhand, possibly exposing a weak area.

When the woman is at the net, she should have her racket up and be alert

89

Figure 39   Classic mixed doubles positions. Kim Yun Ja of South Korea, partnered by Park Joo Bong, trying to maintain the attack with a half-court push

Figure 40   Another South Korean pair, Kim Moon Soo and Hwang Hye Yung, show the classic serving positions for mixed doubles

and dominating. She should aim to maintain, or gain, the attack whenever possible by playing the shuttle in a downward direction, by net shots or by delicate pushes into the mid-court area between the opposing players. When the shuttle is high and the opposition is about to attack, the woman should cover the cross-court shot.

If the man has an opportunity to attack, it is often effective to smash at the opposing woman or to drop straight in front of the opposing man – so bringing him in to the net.

When the man is serving, the woman usually stands in front of him on his backhand side (see figure 40). She should stay as central as possible but must give her partner a clear track to serve. This can be achieved if she keeps her feet fairly central and leans her body to the side.

Training

Playing badminton is a very enjoyable way of becoming fitter, and many people will not have the time or inclination to undertake any additional training. However, physical fitness is as important a component of a player's ability as his shot production.

It is important to warm-up and warm-down when training or playing. Stretching is a vital component of physical fitness: it should never be neglected and can be readily incorporated into your warm-up and warm-down routines.

Stamina can be improved by steady pace runs of 40-60 minutes. You should feel comfortable throughout the run. The aim of this training is to increase aerobic fitness. If you push yourself too hard you are training anaerobically, which is not the intention. At the end of the run you should feel mildly tired, *not* exhausted. If you decide to do some running, then remember:

1. If in any doubt about your fitness, have a medical check-up first.
2. Start with short runs and build up *very* gradually; walk parts of the run if necessary.

3. Try to breathe deeply but comfortably throughout the exercise.
4. Wear suitable running shoes with plenty of cushioning.
5. If you begin to develop aches or pains, see a physiotherapist.

Another excellent way to improve stamina is to swim. This has the great advantage of putting minimal strain on joints and muscles whilst still training the cardio-vascular system.

Apart from steady-state running, the Steve Baddeley programme contains a wide range of training exercises: track running (mainly sequences of 400 metres), sprinting, skipping, circuit training, weight training, jump circuits, and various fast-foot-movement exercises.

However, your time to train may be limited, and so, apart from the stamina training already mentioned, the rest of your fitness training may be better undertaken on a badminton court. That can be done with 'shadow badminton'.

This involves shadowing or copying badminton movements without a shuttle. Start on the base, move to the front right-hand corner, shadowing a forehand net shot, and then return to the base. This can be repeated ten times at a slow comfortable pace, or five times with more explosion.

Alternatively, build up the sequence to incorporate a smash followed by a net shot. Or, use all four corners by moving from one to another via the base, in a clockwise pattern. The variations are limitless.

The advantage of this form of training is that it is very specific. Not only are you training your body physically, but you are also practising and improving your footwork patterns and stroke actions.

Badminton fitness can also be improved by undertaking sequence training. This involves at least two players – one feeding and one working – and in these exercises you will be hitting shuttles, so improving your stroke production as well as your fitness. The feeder hits the shuttle in a pre-arranged pattern, and the worker returns the shuttle to the feeder's position.

Once again there are a large number of possibilities. Common, and very useful, sequences are the worker playing a drop shot, followed by a net shot, followed by a drop shot, etc. The feeder stays at the net lifting the first shot and playing a net shot on the next, and so on. You can change the drop shot for a smash.

Postscript

The advice in these pages should be a guide and not a blueprint. If it can be taken that way there is every chance the reader will end up becoming more skilful at badminton. He or she should also enjoy it more.

In the fullest sense, though, it will not make a complete player. Badminton is a sport, which implies it is based not only upon competition but upon cooperation. There are fundamental areas that cannot be legislated for or taught by rules of the game or coaching guidelines. If players cannot cooperate and agree on values of fairness and decency that underlie it, then it ceases to be a sport at all. And eventually the whole magnificient edifice will corrode from within.

To be a complete player, therefore, means also to have a love of the underlying purposes of the game and a respect for the ethical considerations that helped create it. It means to appreciate the concord that can be made between very different types of people. It means to behave well. It means not knowingly to cheat.

There is no reason why men and women should not play the game hard, without quarter given, and to the limit of the rules. There is no reason why some of them should not earn money from it, occasionally very good money. The professional and the old amateur ideals are by no means completely incompatible.

It is true these ideals have been in conflict in many sports. Badminton, more than most, has been able to retain a wonderful spirit between players whilst making progress towards greater wealth and higher standards. This may or may not continue. It will depend upon the attitudes and character of the players of the future. To them this book is dedicated.